Dawn FLiGHT

A Lakota STORY

Once, a girl and her father went hiking and saw an eagle flying overhead.
The father was so excited to see the magnificent bird that he changed
the course of their journey to follow it.

His daughter asked him why they were following the eagle, and her father started to tell her a story. "This is a story passed down by your ancestors for many years," he began.

"There was a time when the people who roamed these lands were not good to one another. There was great unhappiness that spread across these hills and valleys like a disease."

6

"But not everyone was bad. Some people were good to others.
And of all of these people, one woman stood out as the most virtuous.
She was kind and pure of heart."

"One day a flood came to cleanse and renew the Earth. The skies went dark, and a deafening clap of thunder echoed through the valley. The rain began to fall as if it would never stop."

"The good people gathered together and called upon tȟuŋkášila, the Grandfather above. They asked him to see and hear what was noble in the people of his land and to save the kindness in their hearts."

The Grandfather listened, and was forgiving. He transformed the kind people into the soft stone that fills the quarries near Pipestone, Minnesota. Then he turned the rebellious people into the hard Sioux Quartzite to cover and protect the soft stone."

"There was only one survivor of the human race—that kind and virtuous woman. The Grandfather heard the call of the good people and spared her from the flood, sending a mighty golden eagle down to rescue her."

"From the skies came the loud sound of beating wings. Waŋblí, the eagle swooped down towards the woman. He lifted her up with his strong talons and carried her away with his mighty wings."

"They flew to the only thing that stood above the flooded Earth, čhaŋwákȟaŋ, the Great Tree of Life. It was a gift from the Grandfather — a magnificent tree full of energy and vitality that connected the Earth with the spirit world."

"At the Great Tree of Life, the woman knew that she was safe. And, as the sun came out, she watched the flood slowly begin to disappear. It was a new beginning."

"From his perch on the tree, the eagle made a shrill call.
The woman knew he was talking to her and understood
what he said, as easily as you understand me speaking to you.
The eagle visited the woman each day and taught her to live a good life."

"The magnificent bird had as many teachings as it had feathers! From these feathers, the woman learned about truthfulness, kindness, generosity, respect, and courage. The Eagle explained that each of these feathers helped him to fly. And through these virtues, mankind could soar."

From the woman, a new race came to the Earth. Every day, she prepared a meal for her family and passed on the knowledge that the eagle had given her. Each time the people followed these lessons, it carried them above the problems and darkness of the world, like eagle wings."

"The people grew into a race that was made of one people and spread around the Earth from the plains to the mountains. They are your ancestors—they learned to be patient and kind, and they cared deeply for the land."

"Each time the people saw the eagle flying ahead, they saw the bird's broad wings and were reminded to live a life according to the eagle's teachings."

"Today I recognize the spirit of the eagle in myself, and in you,"
the father told his daughter, as the eagle soared above them.
"Like the eagle, we must learn to always fly towards the light."

As the father finished his story, the two found themselves in a clearing. No sooner had they stopped to admire the view when an eagle feather came floating from the sky and landed at the girl's feet.

The girl picked up the feather and held it up to her father. "Little one!" he said, "The eagle wanted you to have one of his feathers. This is a great blessing!"

The girl was so excited that she wanted to
go home at once to show her mother.

When she had shown the feather to her family and her friends, the girl put it in her bedroom, where she could look at it every day. She promised to recognize the eagle in herself and others and always to soar above the darkness, into the light.

Conversation Starters:

- What do you think you can do to be more like the eagle?

- Have you ever seen an eagle? What did it look like?

- How many feathers do you think a golden eagle has?

- What do the words virtuous and noble mean?

- Who do you know who is virtuous and noble?

- Did you see the talking feather in the story?

- What happens when you hold a talking feather?

Dear reader,

The part of the story in which the virtuous people's sincere prayers reach the sky and are answered by being changed into Čhaŋnúŋpa Ša (Catlinite or Pipestone) instead of being swept away and destroyed in the deluge, refers to one of the most important North American archeological sites; Čhaŋnúŋp-ok'é / the Pipestone Quarry near Pipestone, MN. Because this unique soft, deep red stone symbolizes how heavenly influences create beauty, oneness, and heavenly virtues in human hearts, Pipestone Quarry has been a place of pilgrimage for countless generations.

May your hearts soar on wings of spirit,
Kevin Locke

A Book of Medicine Wheel Education

Books for ages 7-12 (available in English and French)

Educational lesson plans and posters
available online!